TAD

ALSO BY PAUL ROMAINE

Up The Down Ladder of Success

Up The Down Ladder of Success

Essential Hidden Traits that Singers and Songwriters
Need for Success in their Music

Paul Romaine

TAD Publications
New Hampshire, USA

Up The Down Ladder of Success

TAD Publications books may be purchased for educational, business, or sales promotional use. Some are available at special discounts for bulk purchases. TAD Publications also publishes books in electronic formats. For further information you can write to them at:

CustomerService@tadpublications.com

Paperback ISBN: 978-0-9886580-0-4
E-Book ISBN: 978-0-9886580-1-1

First Paperback Edition

Printed in the "United States of America"

This book is dedicated to the spirit of STEVE JOBS who never gave up searching for excellence through his creativity and persistence.

It is also for the strong determination of all the singers, songwriters, and musicians that struggle to climb back *Up the Down Ladder of Success.*

Contents

PART THREE

PART FOUR

Music That Warms Our Emotional Hearts

By *Paul Romaine*

When we look in on an infant child asleep in bed and see his/her total innocence as Brahms' Lullaby "Go to Sleep" plays on the music box.

When we see a beautiful, large flag with rich red, white and blue stripes as it is waving in a warm breeze. And then we hear "America the Beautiful" and the words 'O beautiful for spacious skies, For amber waves of grain, For purple mountain majesties, Above the fruited plain!'

When that special moment happens when a man and a woman look into each other's eyes and realize they have fallen in love while listening to a romantic song like "Only You and You Alone."

When two people are at a Rock & Roll concert listening to songs that they know the words to and are having a marvelous time tapping there hands or feet to the beat of the music. Oh What a Night!

When a large family gathering is together at Christmas time and they decide to sing carols like "Jingle Bells," "Santa Claus Is Coming To Town" and "Silent Night." Memories of their own childhood warm their hearts.

Introduction

This book's title *Up the Down Ladder of Success* says a lot about persistence and never giving up. You may fall down the 'Up Ladder' from time to time but Failure only happens if you do nothing and give up.

I came across a You Tube video of a conference with Steve Jobs and Bill Gates. In a question and answer segment a member of the audience asked Steve this question. "What is the most valuable piece of advice you could give to entrepreneurs that are attempting to make their projects successful"? If you will forgive me for paraphrasing here, Steve's advice was this. 'The most important thing you should have is passion in what you are doing. Trying to achieve success is so hard and you have to do it over a sustained period of time. When setbacks occur if you do not love what you are doing and you are not passionate about it, you're going to give up and that is what happens to most people'.

In this book you're going to learn about hidden traits that are important in a music career but are rarely if ever a part of a school's curriculum.

This is not to say that schools of music do not offer a good variety of music courses. They do. However the reading material that you are about to embark on is the perfect complement to a full, formal music education or as a stand alone informational product for artists pursuing a different course in their music career.

Some of the chapter titles provide a glimpse into their contents such as: Creating a unique sound vocally or instrumentally, Truthfully defining your idea of Success in a career path, Studying your craft, Singing versus screeching, Software that adjusts your dysfunctional tone or pitch – admit it you have a problem, Work attitude, Manners, Your music and the internet and much more.

In closing I hope that as you immerse yourself into this prescription for success you will be excited as you enhance your learning experience. It's these extra hidden or forgotten things that add to your being an all-around better artist.

I so much appreciate your joining me in exploring the wonderful world of music and wish you much success.

Take good care,

Paul

Part One

"Study constantly"

1

Success: Defining Your Career Path

One of the most important things for an artist to do is to define what he or she considers being successful in music means. Remember now, we are talking about what YOU consider success to be for yourself not what other people consider success is and there is a big difference here.

Some folks would label success as being a superstar. The chances of becoming a superstar are slim. However this does not mean one should give up the dream.

Others would feel that if they play in a band on a regular basis and perform mainly on weekends at various clubs and they get paid for doing so then that means success for them.

I know some celebrity artists that say money is not the most important thing to them. Even if they weren't well known and didn't get much money for performing, as long as they could play their music and sing their songs they would be happy.

One such artist was a country singer named Marty Robbins. Marty had a lot of hits and even though he passed away in 1982 at the age of 57 his music lives on to this day. Some of his hits were "A White Sport Coat and a Pink Carnation," "El Paso," "My Woman, My Woman, My Wife" and "Don't Worry."

Many other singers commented over the years how Marty just loved to sing. And even if he wasn't scheduled to perform he would do so at the drop of a hat. Even during a regular show he would often go way over the allotted time if the audience wanted him to keep singing because he just loved to sing and perform.

Other artists that have commented how money was not the most important thing for performing were Willie Nelson, Merle Haggard, and Roger Miller. The thing that does top their list is having the opportunity to sing and play music because fans are interested in seeing and hearing them perform.

Last year I happened to be a guest on a radio show along with Danny Nova. Danny's background is superb in that he is a contemporary rock recording artist who plays 10 instruments and has a 4 plus octave vocal range. In November of 2008 he headlined at Carnegie Hall in New York. The concert received rave reviews and ongoing press about his success.

Danny defines himself as an acoustic singer and songwriter with a modern blues, slightly folksier twist.

He has powerful vocals that originate from a rock opera, concert type background. Symphonic overtones are present that appeal to varied music enthusiasts.

As we were being interviewed and during conversations we had on the show we began to realize that we had a lot in common in regards to music and thought alike on certain issues.

As Danny said I am living the American Dream. I do not feel like some artists do that it's a competition between us singers or that I have to top my performance with something always new to stay ahead of the pack. I'm interested in playing and singing my music and love doing it whenever I can.

The common thread between Danny and me is that he is a singer, songwriter, and musician and I am a writer, broadcaster, and interviewer of celebrity music artists. The wonderful thing about this thread is that we love music so much and could talk for hours about it. He's a man I'm proud to call my friend.

Danny is also an advocate for the Music and Arts Foundation in America. The organization provides tuition scholarships for music and arts students. It also provides grants for enrichment programs at public, private and charter schools.

As you have seen there are differing opinions as to what some people consider Success. This is why it's important for you to determine what your specific idea is for success and write that thought down on paper. Hopefully that does not sound too juvenile but I cannot emphasize it enough.

Whether you're just starting a music career or are currently performing in some way or another, the first thing that you must do is Define Your Career Path and put it down on paper.

That doesn't mean you can't change course along the way but it's critical that you start out with the above first step in a definitive plan and work from there.

If you are just starting out there are some things you should check out if you want to join a band and play some small venues even if some of them are dives and you will be working for short money.

- The first thing would be to go see the band perform. If done anonymously then that is all the better.
- Some of the questions that you should ask yourself in regards to your endeavor would be what's the makeup of the band in terms of musicians, instruments and lead singer?
- Most importantly how do they sound?
- How many bookings are they getting and how often are they working?
- How much are you paid and on what basis? For example are you paid a flat fee, or if there's a cover charge does the band get a percentage of that?
- Is the band allowed to sell its products and does the club owner get a cut of that? When do you get paid?

- How much traveling do you have to do? Are there any associated costs that you have to contribute to that?

Once that's accomplished and if you decide to join the band would you then be satisfied with your success and just continue along that path? If that is the case and you are comfortable with that then good for you.

Please remember that these are only a sampling of the questions you need to plan out and ask. Not all of them might apply but doing this exercise causes you to be aware of all the planning it takes to pursue a career.

I realize that this seems like a chore laying it out and all. But once it's done then you've always got that as a guide. You'd be surprised how many people make career choices and do not give much thought as to how they're going to accomplish their goals.

If on the other hand you wanted to move on to other avenues in music that is OK also. But again you will have to lay it all out and then try to follow the new plan.

Your Notes

Your Notes

2

Study Your Craft and Experiment

Another trait that is so important for an artist to have but is seldom discussed is to STUDY YOUR CRAFT. Now this does not mean study as in taking lessons to play an instrument or classes in Music Theory as is given in music schools.

It means the hidden things like having an abundance of curiosity for all things regarding music. Remember the more things that you know the more successful you will be. This not only applies to music but to any job.

If we look at all the great baseball players over time we see that they lived and breathed baseball day in and day out. They gave and accomplished way more than a 100% effort because they studied their profession to the ultimate level.

And so in terms of music I am going to give you some examples of celebrities who always had the urge to study their craft and this way you will get an idea of what I am talking about.

The first one is Frank Sinatra. There was a documentary about him and in one section it told how Frank who was already a mega-star did the following. He went to visit his friend, the opera singer Pavarotti for some advice. He needed to know how, when singing Pavarotti managed to hold with clarity a certain syllable in a word. Pavarotti told him how it was done.

What made this notable is that Frank was not embarrassed to ask. He took his craft seriously and simply went to another singer to see what the answer was as to how to do something involving musical clarity.

Another singer is Lady Gaga. She had been taking piano lessons from the age of four. At age 11 she was set to join the Julliard School in Manhattan, but instead attended the Convent of the Sacred Heart, a private Roman Catholic school. She went on to write her first piano ballad at 13 and began performing at Open Mic nights at age 14. At 17 she gained early admission to New York University's Tisch School of the Arts. While there she studied music and improved her songwriting skills.

James Phillips, a music director and one of her early mentors noticed her in the fifth grade as a talented singer. As the years progressed he continued to be her mentor and teach her in musical performances and jazz at Regis High School in New York.

When she was 17 another teacher Pam Philips had a vocal technique class that she gave at NYU. It was titled the CAP 21 program and said that her student was hitting high notes as a soprano with an impressive vocal range. She also said that she was very unique in how she dressed and stood out in her dance classes.

During Pam's classes one could see Lady Gaga's insatiable appetite for music knowledge. This was apparent when she asked Pam how to use her voice for pop music by learning how to take 50s and 60s vocals and apply them to contemporary music.

Along with everything else, Gaga has embraced the world of fashion since it is a major factor in her act. Donatella Versace is considered her source of inspiration when it comes to creating fashion. Gaga tries to soak up as much knowledge as possible for designing all her costumes and hair designs.

I specifically chose these two artists so that you could see how they meticulously 'Studied their Craft.' One of them was a seasoned veteran singer and a legend (Sinatra). The other is a very good singer who is a megastar (Gaga). Their knack for always looking to learn more and as much as possible about their profession certainly enhanced their careers as artists.

It does one's heart good to hear or read a story about an artist, producer, or studio engineer who experiments with a song to create a certain effect.

One person is Sam Phillips, the founder of the legendary Sun Records. In a documentary about 'Sun' he stated that when starting out he would try different intros and other things that eventually worked musically.

As he said, basically we didn't know any better but we were willing to try different things musically and see how it sounded.

One of the reasons that such renowned artists at Sun like Elvis Presley, Carl Perkins, Johnny Cash and Jerry Lee Lewis became what they were was they had a special talent. Beyond that they were intent on recording a good product and were willing to experiment.

Another creative person was Jerry Wexler. He is the man who created the term Rhythm & Blues when he did a stint at Billboard Magazine.

He also worked at various record companies one of which was Atlantic Records. Jerry wore different hats at Atlantic. He was an A&R man but quite often produced several celebrity singers in the recording studio. Eventually Bobby Darin came in to record a song titled "Splish Splash."

Wexler wanted to add the sound of water splashing and with a stroke of creativity did the following. He simply took a container, filled it with water, put a microphone near it, and wiggled the tips of his fingers in the water. And hence when you listened to the record, the sound of the water splashing to simulate someone taking a bath is Jerry's experimenting to get what he hoped would sound right and it did.

There are two schools for learning music. One is the education in the class room and the other is the education of learning from other artists on life's music highway.

Your Notes

Your Notes

3

Persistence: Never Give Up

The question that is frequently asked of singers and other artists who are constantly trying to get recognition is "Why after being rejected do you constantly keep trying to finally get acknowledgment of your work?" And the most common answer is "Because I love what I am doing and want to do it for a career."

Recently this was evident with actor Eric Stonestreet's acceptance speech after winning an Emmy for Best Supporting Actor in the "Modern Family" television show at the 2012 Emmy awards.

He said "he wanted to share the award with every actor out there who has an audition tomorrow at 5 o'clock in Santa Monica. I've went to every one of them and never missed one and I'm living proof that if you do that and stick to your craft and be motivated and positive you can stand up here before all you beautiful people."

Eric's comments were certainly a testament to keep trying and if you do not give up you can succeed.

Another similar event was on a previous season of American Idol. Jennifer Lopez and Steven Tyler were talking to some of the contestants who were not quite good enough to be chosen but had promise if they came back in a year or so and tried again.

Jennifer and Steven both said that when they were starting out in the entertainment business they got rejected several times. But they never gave up on trying out for spots that were available on particular shows and how important it is for the contestants to be persistent.

Another situation that goes back quite a few years with a similar story is about Kris Kristofferson.

Kris was struggling as a songwriter while working as a janitor at the legendary Sun Records. He was always trying to get anyone that would listen to record one of his songs.

When Johnny Cash was at Sun doing some recording work, the management at Sun told Kris not to be bothering Johnny about songs he had written.

But Kris never wanting to miss an opportunity from time to time would slip one of his songs to one of Johnny's assistants to give to Johnny and see if he was interested in recording it. Kris would never get much of a response and the typical reply was that Johnny hadn't got to it yet.

Along Kris's life journey he got some training as a helicopter pilot as he had some of that experience in the military. Even though he was frustrated at Sun, he was determined to get one of his songs to Johnny. So lo and behold what does he do? He gets a helicopter and flies over to Johnny's house and lands right on the back yard lawn.

Obviously people including Johnny came out of the house and someone asked "What's going on here?" And Kris said to Johnny, 'I'm a songwriter and I've been trying to get one of my songs that I've written to you to see if there is any interest in it. Up till now I haven't had much success.'

Johnny did take the song and said that he would take a look at it. One has to wonder what went through Johnny's mind after a guy lands a helicopter in his back yard and wants him to take a look at one of his compositions. My guess is that he had to admit what happened was different but A+ for Kris's creativity.

In any event a couple of weeks passed and Kris got word that Johnny was going to record Kris's song. Its title was "Sunday Mornin' Comin' Down" and it did become a big hit.

Kris Kristofferson is one of my all time favorite songwriters. His many hit songs that were written since then like "For the Good Times," "Me and Bobby McGee," "Help Me Make It Through the Night," and "Why Me" along with so many others will live on for many years to come.

The three examples I have talked about here can pretty much apply to any career although to do the ultimate scenario such as the one with Johnny perhaps requires along with persistence a little bit of insanity.

None the less they are living proof that if you don't give up and keep pursuing your hopes and dreams they can come true.

There's another situation here that needs clarification Quite often parents or family relatives will say things to discourage a person from trying to accomplish something in music.

If you know you've got what it takes then don't give up. It's very tough to keep up your spirits when family gets involved in a negative way. Your motivation can get shot down so low but stay focused.

In a slightly different light I have seen singers say that they owe a lot to a parent or relative who believed in them and encouraged them to keep trying. It really does not matter if you are a boy or a girl, young or old, tall or short, man or woman or where you're from because you do have a chance.

There is also a related situation when having had exposure to rejection early on and having survived is a good thing in helping you to deal with it down the road.

Take an artist whose first four single records were pretty much flops. The singer still feels that he/she can do well if one can find the right song to get some momentum going Up the Down Ladder of Success.

Or what about an artist that has been in the music business and had some songs that charted but still did not break the Top 20 list. He or she just needs that one hit song to accomplish more.

In the above two scenarios if one had experienced stumbling blocks early on in their careers hopefully there were lessons learned at that time on how to deal with it now regarding their career.

Your Notes

Your Notes

4

Work Ethic

The amount of ethics one applies to any situation, the better will be the results.

The work ethic refers to one's moral principles. In other words if a person has good ethics then it means that he/she tries to do the right thing in doing a good job.

Examples of this would be when an employee tries to be on time for the start of the work day, does not take long periods of breaks, and is not taking a lot of days off.

Quite often we hear of someone saying that a person has a good work ethic or 'boy, he/she is one hard working person.' Obviously this is important for singers and musicians to have. If you do then you will have the respect of all folks that are part of the show. You owe it to them to be on time, know your material, and the stage layout.

Each person is part of a team for the show. The musicians, singers, lighting people, stage and equipment set-up are all dependent on each other.

There have been times that I have been to a concert and the opening band comes out to do all their sound checks and instrument checks before they perform their part of the show.

The problem here is that if the band takes too long to do this the audience gets bored. Sound checks that take forever are boring and the audience is there to be entertained. Here's a good example of why these things should be planned out beforehand.

The concert I went to was a George Jones show. The opening act did all their checks and finally got to the point of starting their part of the show. Remember there is no value in seeing them tuning their instruments.

After intermission the George Jones band came out, took their positions at their instruments and kicked it off right away. Several people in the audience said 'ooh and ahs.' And of course the reason for this response is that the sound checks done in advance were right on tune and the audience knew that they were being entertained right from the start of George's show. Now one might say that Jones' equipment was top of the line as compared to an opening band's but the fact be told the opening band could have done a better job of being prepared.

The above example is just another hidden trait that's not very often talked about but is important. Whether you are some small two piece band or a medium sized group of musicians, professionalism should be at the top of your list. If it's not there then you will not get noticed as well.

Remember the audience. They are not singers or musicians but they know when someone has their act together.

I want to give you a couple of celebrity artists that are most assuredly as hard working as one can get. One is from back in the day and another is one who is current.

First up is a lady known as 'The Singing Rage,' Miss Patti Page. She has sold over 100 million records. There was one period in time when she was cranking out 250+ singing dates in a year. As a singer she has covered many venues of work.

As time went on she also ventured into television and had a highly rated and popular show. She even ventured into movies including "Elmer Gantry" and "Boys Night Out" along with a busy tour schedule.

Even though the television shows were short usually averaging 15 minutes or a ½ hour, much preparation had to be done. Her day would begin by being up at 5:30 in the morning, going to the studio, doing some makeup, rehearsing songs, and doing interviews with writers.

After a long day at the television studio she would then have meetings at the recording studio for promotional duties tied in with her recordings. She would be in bed late in the evening and up again early the next morning for a similar busy day.

To say she was a hard worker is an understatement. It takes a lot of stamina to persevere and grind out a schedule like that.

The other person who is more currently known and truly a super-star is Lady Gaga. As with Patti she is a workaholic.

She could be up early in the morning, out doing promos at radio stations all day, lunches and dinner meetings with music business reps and playing clubs at night.

She would then go back to the hotel and be up early the next day to get on the next flight to the next town and repeat the same routine. This type of schedule could go on for weeks with her getting as little as four hours of sleep a night if lucky.

The woman has a 'can do' in spades. I saw her in a video where she took a fall off the top of her piano and when hitting the deck on her back was still singing the song as she got up to recoup and finish the number.

As we look at these two women's work ethic we see that even though they had made it to the heights as recording artists they never gave up on working hard at their career.

Now this does not mean to say that one has to go to those extremes in their own career. It could even be argued that the higher one goes in their career then the harder one must work and increase their promotional work as necessary.

Simply put, if they can work that hard after reaching star status, then even if you're in a small band you should also develop a good work ethic for yourself.

Your Notes

Your Notes

5

Etiquette: It Does Make A Difference

This is another hidden trait that is important but is seldom discussed. I'm going to tell you a personal story about its importance. Then I'm going to tell you about a music industry giant named Berry Gordy, the founder of Motown Records and his thinking about etiquette.

From a personal point of view my mother always tried to teach me about etiquette. She certainly knew something about it as she was a maid and nanny for wealthy people. She was poor by most standards but was rich in being a good mother and holding our family together.

She would constantly harp when we ate our meals at home with information like "Paul, you should hold your fork like this or Paul when you eat those Parker House rolls you should break them like this.' Sadly as a typical teenager what she said to me did not sink in too well. Also I just could not understand why she was always bugging me about that stuff.

After high school I enlisted in the service in the U.S. Marine Corps. After a year or so, the Marines had managed to eliminate the teenager in me and my thinking as a young man began to look at life differently.

I decided to purchase a book on Etiquette which was through "Esquire", a magazine for men. Up to that time mostly all the etiquette books were written for women. Those books were excellent but what made the Esquire book appealing is that it was written in a man's lingo.

My dear mother was obviously elated knowing that there was still hope for me in learning some of the finer points of behavior in life.

Years later when my son was a young man I told him the importance of it all. I said to him that it wasn't so much the practicing of etiquette to the letter of the law but at least knowing what is proper.

I mentioned how it could be important in one's job or in an interview or in doing business with someone for this reason.

If the person you are talking to doesn't have any etiquette then it doesn't make any difference if you do or not. Ignorance is bliss. But if the person you are talking with does have good etiquette and you don't, they could be turned off by it and it could mean a missed opportunity for any number of things.

That said, think of the music industry. There are some brash people in it and again in that instance it does not make any difference. On the other hand there are people in it that are polished such as some of the club owners, other singers, musicians, and executives in events and in television. You would be amazed how some of them would go the extra distance if they knew that you were a stand-up person who has some values.

Well that's my personal story. Now I would like to talk with you about Berry Gordy. He was the founder of Motown records, one of the most successful record companies that produced so many star singers and groups.

Imagine being responsible for celebrities like Stevie Wonder, The Temptations, Smokey Robinson, The Four Tops, Diana Ross and The Supremes, Martha Reeves and the Vandellas, Marvin Gaye, The Miracles, The Jackson 5, Gladys Knight and the Pips, Lionel Richie, and so many more.

Motown was a family run business. Gwen and Anna Gordy ran Artist Development. They hired Maxine Powell who ran an agency of models to work with their artists.

When Powell arrived she knew she had her work cut out for her. Some of the singers were really rough on the edges. Rudeness abounded with them but the singers were hard workers.

When Motown made it mandatory that they take a daily two-hour class the ones that were serious about their music education took it.

Everything was covered including proper table manners, dressing to show a professional appearance with hat and gloves, learning the importance of good posture, personal hygiene, learning how a lady should properly get in and out of a car. Mary Wilson of the Supremes felt that the group had more self-confidence and that other people began treating them differently.

Even male groups got some polishing up. The Four Tops were taught how to move on stage, dress, walk and talk to reporters.

Choreography was taught to several acts by professionals and the improvement in their acts was noticeable in a heartbeat.

Imagine the education that all these singers got by being with Motown. While many other record companies were content to have singers who could make a hit record, Motown took it all a step further.

If you polish the acts including not just their singing and music but also their etiquette then that is the ultimate sparkle on their behavior that anyone could ask for.

Ask anyone at Motown that was responsible for developing the artists if they did it right and with pride they would say we groomed them well. And the artists knew that they were part of a company that would have its place as a legendary hit maker in music.

Your Notes

Your Notes

Part Two

"The Other Side of the Coin"

6

Screeching versus Singing and Hocus-pocus Pitch

There are two things in music that when I hear them are a thorn in my side.

The first is screeching rather than singing. Now in this case I am not referring to the screeching in heavy rock bands. In that case it's almost expected to hear a vocalist doing that as part of the show.

What I am referring to is ballads and other pop hits when the singer moves up the register by an octave and will attempt to hit the high notes.

Very few singers can hit the high notes with musical clarity and tone. Sadly screeching is the norm. Even current singers that are performing often fit the slot of screeching rather than singing. It seems that even the Talent Show judges wow when some of the contestants reach up to hit the note. How they can view the incident with wow when there is no tone or pitch but plenty of hollering is beyond my comprehension.

In recent years the perfect example of someone that could do it all was Whitney Houston. She proved she can hit the notes bringing it on up with perfect pitch and tone with that commercial voice of hers.

The song that showcases that extraordinary voice of hers is "I Will Always Love You" written by Dolly Parton. It was on the Original Soundtrack album from the movie *The Bodyguard* starring Kevin Costner.

At one point the record had sold 40 million copies and was certified 17x Platinum by the Recording Industry Association of America in 1990.

Going back much further another singer that could put it altogether was Dusty Springfield. This is shown when she cranks it up in her recording of "You Don't Have to Say You Love Me." Tone perfect, pitch right on, and that commercial voice of hers bringing it on home. Part way through the song she boosts it up an octave and you do say wow and it is much deserved by this brilliant singer.

Now, there are good singers who cannot hit the high notes with clarity but they are smart enough to correct the situation.

If a singer is good when they approach the high note they do the following. They do not hold it for a long period of time and even reduce the strength of the note or drop it down a half. Smart singers can do that.

A very good singer that comes to mind is Lisa Layne. She recorded the 7th most requested Christmas song of all time. It's "All I Want for Christmas is You" with Vince Vance and the Valiants. Bragging rights are allowed when it gets that much airplay.

Lisa has a distinctive commercial voice and in the original version of All I Want for Christmas, when she gets to the high notes she handles them beautifully.

Lisa has an album out called "Shades of Blue" that has a lot of great songs on it. It is available in Amazon's MP 3 section. As a whole I really like the album but a few of my favorite hits are "Dreamer", "Misty Blue" and "You Don't Know Me."

The other sore spot that aggravates me is artists that use what I call Hocus-pocus with pitch by using various types of software to alter their voice recording for pitch and other sorts of modifications.

I personally view this in the same light as Baseball players who are juicing and because of it have extra power for hitting home runs. The same is true for Olympic athletes in various contests especially in Track and Field. When the head lines come out and state that he or she is the fastest person ever, one begins to wonder is it real or is it steroids and all. There have been documented cases of athletes that have lost their awards due to this.

In sports most of these situations can be tracked. If an athlete performs for several years in a standard fashion and then all of a sudden they are cranking the ball out of the park like never before, common sense tells you that something is up.

My feelings are if you've got to modify your abilities in order to so something that you are not normally capable of doing then you do not deserve any awards. You either have it or you don't.

And if you win an award whether it be in sports (Trophies for Best, Most, Fastest) or in music awards for singing (Grammy or otherwise) and it was done by changing the norm then you do not deserve it. In music if you use software to adjust your dysfunctional pitch, tone or anything else, admit it you have a problem.

For singers that can sing naturally, we know they can. I'll give you two examples of ordinary people that I've heard.

One is my wife. She does not have any desire to sing professionally and never goes any further than Karaoke with a band at one of the local clubs. But she can sing. At times in the house I will hear her singing with a song that's playing on the radio or singing a song she likes, a cappella. No flat notes, no pitch problems, just pure singing tone. When one has it, they have it. It is immediately recognizable.

Another example, I was in a store shopping a while back and as I was in one aisle I could hear a woman softly humming in the next aisle to a song that was playing over the radio in the store. Again no flat notes, no pitch problems, and pure singing.

Singing that looks you right in the eye and embraces you with its beauty.

That's how it is folks. What a joy it is to my ears to hear someone sing that can really sing.

I love our music profession so much. There are some songs that are so beautiful that they can bring tears to my eyes. These types of songs are made by real singers and the quality shines through as a beacon of beauty.

Your Notes

Your Notes

7

Talent Shows: Pluses and Minuses

Amazingly enough there are even hidden traits that require thought if a person desires to try out for the major Talent Shows on television.

After you read all the Pros and Cons below, you should ask yourself "How bad do I want to get on the show?" Remember wanting it is one thing but making it happen is something else altogether.

Many people are willing to travel hundreds of miles with very little cash and sleep to get to the audition site to apply. On top of that, the process is lengthy.

On the plus side one gets a maximum amount of exposure especially if you are in the Top 12 contestants left standing and vying for a top spot of 1st, 2nd, or 3rd place.

On the negative side your chances are extremely limited and slim to ever get into the Top 12 positions let alone winning the top spot in the competition. Eventually you're competing with the best of the best, so if you do not think you're in that group you will not get very far.

And also the pluses and minuses are given here for you to give serious thought to the things that are not so evident.

For example, one does not realize that even out of all the Number 1 contest winners over the years, very few of those really succeed in becoming a superstar much less having decent record sales. Winning the contest does not necessarily mean that along with the record deal one is going to have any hit records. And believe me when I say that a career can really tank quite rapidly if recordings do not have anything substantial to offer as time goes on.

On March 10, 2011 Kid Rock was a guest on the Piers Morgan Show. He and Piers were talking about American Idol and Kid Rock had felt that Steven Tyler had sold out by taking a judging position on the show. He and Steven are good friends so this was not said in a malicious manner.

Kid Rock told Piers that he felt these shows do not mentor the contestants enough. He felt that for one to become a success in singing as a profession they have to get a lot more experience than a stint on a Talent Show.

He mentioned that he and his father always had a good relationship while he was growing up. I believe he mentioned that his father had a garage to fix cars. Kid Rock explained that his dad always tried to instill in him a good work ethic and it served him well in regards to his own career.

His father had told him when he was growing up to remember that "before you can own the garage you've got to know how to sweep the floor." And so this was said in the context of the contestants on Talent shows not having the amount of time that it takes to learn one's craft really well.

Tony Bennett was another person that felt pretty much the same about shows like American Idol. In June of 2010 he said that Idol fails to teach wannabe stars how to last in the music business.

He told Britain's Newsnight they have the children on Idol and 'They build them up and put them in Wembly Stadium and then they drop them and go on with the next over-dog. The producers are not really treating the young performers right. It takes time for them to learn their craft and how to last'

Unfortunately there are more negatives than positives in one's ability to win a coveted spot on a Talent Show. However for clarification I am not saying to give up on the dream. I am simply saying you need to know about the intricacies of trying to capture a coveted spot on these shows.

Some of the positive things about Talent shows are that viewers get to know more about the judges personally.

When one is a judge we get to hear their comments to the contestants. In some cases we learn things about them that we did not know. We see their understanding of music in their analysis of the singer's rendition and that some judges are really a nice person or some are not or do not have much of a personality.

In terms of the contestants it's nice to hear them tell about their background before going out to perform. In listening to some of their stories one gets to hear some of the heartbreaking struggles they have had to endure. Also to hear about their never give up attitude when trying to accomplish something is truly inspiring.'

There are also some shows that are making progress in the way that a show is laid out. Take "The Voice" for example. The judges can only listen to the contestant sing when he or she begins their audition. They cannot see them until they decide whether they want the singer on their team. This way they cannot see how their stage presence is or if they are young or old et cetera but can only judge them for their singing, This is a great concept in that it's the first thing that should be judged. Can the contestant sing?

Once the judges are interested in bidding for them to be a part of their team they can turn their chairs around and finally get to see the whole package.

"America's Got Talent" is another interesting show. It has proven that a show can be done with different varieties of acts such as singers, magicians, animal acts and the whole nine yards. Variety shows were popular in their time but had vanished decades ago.

AGT does very well in the ratings and deserves much kudos for bringing back a true variety show. They proved all the skeptics wrong by having excellent ratings, good judges, and an entertaining show.

One of the things I wonder about is this. "What's in the air in Britain that so many of the concepts for their talent shows and sitcoms are brought to American audiences?" These shows are exceptionally good shows and the creators of them deserve much credit for bringing their concept successfully to American television.

Your Notes

Your Notes

Part Three

"The Hit-Makers"

8

Songwriters: Lyrics, Song Titles and All

My friend Baker Knight was a songwriter's songwriter. His songs have been recorded by over 40 recording artists starting in 1958 with Rick Nelson's classic hit "Lonesome Town." That was followed by 21 more songs that he wrote for Rick including "There'll Never Be Anyone Else But You" and "I Got a Feelin'."

Besides the hit songs that he wrote for Rick, Baker wrote 11 songs for Dean Martin with the biggest being "Somewhere There's a Someone" and "Nobody's Baby Again."

He also wrote "The Wonder of You" for Elvis Presley which was a Two Million Performance Award winner.

Some of the other artists that recorded hit songs of Baker were Perry Como, Frank Sinatra, Sammy Davis, Jr.

also Mickey Gilley, Hank Williams Jr., Paul McCartney, Bobby Vinton, and Eddy Arnold.

I've always been interested in how songwriters come up with song titles. In a lot of cases it's not a long process. Rather than the writer searching forever, it will just pop up in a conversation and say "Hey here I am. I'm a good title."

To explain further, let me tell you about how the title of a famous Dean Martin song came to Baker.

Baker told me that for "Somewhere There's a Someone" the title came to him while he was standing outside a restaurant in Hollywood waiting for some friends.

There was a convertible car that had to slow down due to traffic as it was passing by. A pretty woman who was driving looked at Baker and smiled.

Now you have to understand that Baker was just an ordinary looking man and he knew that. So he thought to himself, 'imagine a pretty woman like that looking at me and smiling.' The next thought that he had was, 'Good Lord, somewhere there's a someone for everyone.'

See what I mean when I say "It just pops right up at you and says, Here I am." That has happened to me on occasions and most of the time it's when I least expect it.

There's another area of how song titles come about that is different than above. And that is a 'title with a hook.' In other words that title catches your attention by its extended meaning.

For example read these titles and then think of some words that could be attached to the songs:

- The Monster Mash
- That's Amore (When the Moon Hits Your Eyes)
- Shake a Tail Feather
- Gitarzan
- I've Got a Tiger by the Tail
- Zip-a-Dee Doo-Dah
- Chick-a-Boom
- Does Your Chewing Gum Lose Its Flavor
- My Ding-a-Ling
- Who Put the Bomp

The above discussion of song titles is for those of you who are interested in songwriting and want to find good titles.

The last way that a song title comes about is when the writer comes up with it based on the story line of the song. The story line tells what the song is about.

Obviously any discussion of songwriting has to talk about lyrics in general. If one is to be a good songwriter they should be good with the use of words. And they should be especially good with putting groups of words together into phrases.

One of the best ways to see what I am talking about is to look at the phrases that some of the best songwriters have written.

There are legendary writers over the course of history such as Irving Berlin, George Gershwin, Tom T. Hall, Hank Williams, Carole King and Loretta Lynn but I have chosen two whose writing skills are exemplary.

Kris Kristofferson: Kris is one of my favorite songwriters of all time. A lot of folks do not realize that Kris is a Rhodes Scholar who studied Literature at Oxford. His way with phrasing is a study guide in itself. As you read his verses you'll see what I mean.

"For the Good Times"
Lay your head **upon** my pillow
Hold your **warm and tender** body close to mine
Hear the **whisper** of the raindrops
Blow **softly** against my window
Make believe you love me one more time

Now read the lines slowly and think of the words that really convey meaning of calmness, gentleness, and love.
Line one *upon* signifies gently
Line two *warm* and *tender* signifies stimulated body heat
Line three *whisper* signifies peacefulness in the room
Line four *softly* equals calmness
Line five *make believe* are thoughts of how great it once was

The above type of songwriting is a good example of what a great songwriter does with phrasing words. In that case "For the Good Times" is a ballad. But look at what Kris does with a more up tempo song.

"Me and Bobby McGee"
Feelin' flat in Baton Rouge, headin' for the trains
Feelin' nearly faded as my jeans
With them windshield wipers **slappin'** time and
Bobby **clappin'** hands we finally sang up every song that
driver knew
Freedom's just another word for **nothin'** left to lose
And nothin' ain't worth nothin' but it's free
Feelin' good was easy, Lord, when Bobby sang the blues

Notice his use of spelling to signify the way it should be sung, no g's just in'. Songwriting never has to be proper English. Good writers just always want to convey feelings and wording.

Also look at how he conveys a thought in a minimal amount of words. "Feelin' nearly faded as my jeans." In that one thought you realize that those old jeans are as worn as are his emotions.

Again emotions come in to play with windshield wipers slappin' time and Bobby clappin' hands. Yes, it's raining during the drive but they're happy and in a good mood singing songs on the way to their destination.

Freedom's just another word for nothin' left to lose, and nothin' ain't worth nothin' but it's free. This is just simply a play on words but it's catchy in that the listener remembers the words for a long time because its play is unique.

A different type of songwriter was Roger Miller. He was an American singer, songwriter, musician, and actor.

Several artists believed he was a genius when it came to songwriting. This was evident when he composed the music score for a Broadway musical titled *Big River*. He earned a Tony award for "Best Score" of the musical.

Remember when I said that proper English isn't needed when writing a song. This certainly proved to be true with some of Roger's wild and crazy titles and lyrical writing. He had many hit records and deserves to be called a Songwriter's Songwriter.

My main reason for telling you about the very different styles that the above songwriters had when writing their music is that the style doesn't matter as long as it sounds good. This is proven in that they both had several hit records because they were good, so very good!

Your Notes

Your Notes

9

Musicians: Creating a unique and memorable song

Musicians are an important part of any song. The times they really shine are when they create a unique sound. This usually happens if their input is requested or they are asked by the arranger or producer to play it a certain way.

Keeping in mind that studio musicians are the cream of the crop, they can usually produce sounds that any producer or arranger would be proud to have on a recording.

This is one of those hidden traits that you would only get exposure to if you were working with a top name producer, arranger or studio musician. But why not get some exposure to it now so that if you move up to that level you will have some ideas from what you read here.

Since this is a print book you will not be able to click on a link to listen to what I am talking about and it's critical that you hear it.

So as we discuss these artists I will give you the title of the song and the artist. This way you can find it on Amazon or any of the other music sites and listen to it to see what I am describing.

The first song is "Oh Pretty Woman" by Roy Orbison. It was put out by Monument Records and was a big hit.

A unique guitar riff was played at the beginning of the song and even when the song plays today, the riff is still instantly recognizable in identifying the song, "Oh Pretty Woman." Be sure to listen to it and you will understand that unique sound.

Next in terms of guitars is a man who is credited with the twang sound on a guitar. He once was referred to as the Master of Twang. He is Duane Eddy and the song was "Rebel Rouser." If you go into You Tube and find the 2:20 minute version you are there.

Mantovani was known for his swirling violin sounds on his albums. The cascading sound of lush, sweeping violins became known as the Mantovani sound. You can hear this on a song titled "I Wonder Who's Kissing Her Now." It is on his "The Incomparable Mantovani Album."

A man that had a unique style of playing a piano and had a lot of hits was Floyd Cramer. He had a habit of doubling-up two different notes with a slight break at the same time in a measure. Check out the song "Last Date" or "Misty Blue" by Floyd Cramer and you will hear this piano player's instantly recognizable and different style.

Glenn Miller was a band leader whose band toured constantly in the middle of the 20th century and was world renowned. He had searched to create a signature sound for his band and finally found it.

Eventually he began to focus on saxophones in developing the sound. It was finally completed when he used it as part of a song titled "Moonlight Serenade" that he recorded in 1939.

The sound was created by the use of a clarinet-led saxophone section and became his signature theme. Besides 'Serenade' the saxophone sound was evident in songs like "In The Mood", "Little Brown Jug" and many other Miller tunes.

Given that there were many big bands playing during that time Miller's music always stood out on its own with those classic saxophone arrangements.

The last two people I want you to hear about are a songwriter and a singer.

The songwriter is Ellie Greenwich who passed away in 2009. She was one of the premiere song writers working out of the Brill Building in New York City in the 1960s. Ellie's songs garnered 25 gold and platinum records.

As a songwriter she was responsible for creating a sound on one of her hits "Chapel of Love." In an interview she said that while they were working on the song they inserted a hook on one of the words. The word was married. So it sounded like this. Goin' to the chapel and we're gonna get mar-rr-rr-eeed. She said that once she heard the hooked word she knew it was going to be a hit. Dear Ellie was right. It was a hit.

Creating a sound, a hook? It doesn't really matter. AA+ for ingenuity.

The next story concerns Singer Patti Page. She says that when she was recording the song "Confess", at a particular point in the record she would sing the word Confess. Then they felt that another singer would respond with "Confess, Confess" sung in the background.

The problem was they couldn't afford to pay a backup singer. So Patti thought "Maybe I could answer myself in the recording."

Along with the help of the recording engineer they accomplished what they started out to do. Little did they realize that they were making history because on that night she was the first singer to ever double her own voice onto a recording they were making in the studio.

Good Arrangers or Producers can sometimes make a record hit the jackpot in terms of riding up the charts like a bullet when it is released.

Famed Nashville producer Jimmy Bowen was in the process of preliminary preparations for recording a Dean Martin album. The last song to be considered was "Everybody Loves Somebody" which was actually written by Sam Coslow, Irving Taylor, and Ken Lane in 1947. It had been recorded by other artists in the past but no one had any success with it.

Jimmy decided to bring in an Arranger to work on the project. Jimmy told him that he felt that the song should be representative of Dean's style of singing. Smooth and relaxed but still using the full orchestra with back up singers as they had done in some of his other hit recordings.

The end result was that the song was such a hit that it went to Number One on the Billboard charts in 1965 knocking off the Beatles recording of "A Hard Day's Night" which was Number One at the time.

As you can see whether it's a singer, songwriter, musician, A&R man, arranger or producer, just about anyone can wind up contributing some unique element for a song that will make it memorable and a hit. This is an important lesson to be learned as many times it can make a difference in a song's chart success.

Your Notes

Your Notes

10

Raw Talent

I want to include this information on Raw Talent because most singers do not have it and cannot achieve it. This is not to say however that Singers should not study it and use it as a benchmark. There are many good singers out there but Raw Talent is the cream of the crop.

It is rare because this type of talent is so powerful that its magnetism draws you in to an unforgettable experience. Your emotional feelings are extremely heightened by what you are witnessing of the artist's performance. The following story demonstrates it to a tee in the case of a singer that has it in spades. She is Susan Boyle.

In 2009 Susan appeared on the British talent show *Britain's Got Talent*. The song she sang was "I Dreamed a Dream" from the play Les Miserables.

Before she sang one of the judges, Simon Cowell asked her a few background questions. He asked her what was her dream and she said that she wanted to be a professional singer. He then asked her who she would like to be as successful as and Susan said Elaine Page. Elaine is a popular and very talented singer.

Unfortunately when seeing some of the judges' and audience members' facial expressions it was apparent that they had formed an opinion that she would certainly fail her audition. This was based on the fact that she was a middle aged woman who is 47 years old, her appearance as she was plainly dressed, and the way she answered Simon's questions.

When Susan started to sing the first verse of the song the electricity in the audience said it all. The audience began cheering wildly and the expressions on the judges' faces were in awe. Jaws dropped and people realized how wrong they were to have formed an opinion that she would fail.

I've seen a lot of performers over the years and I've seen singers get standing ovations at the end of their performance. Rarely though have I seen what took place during Susan's endearing rendition. Several times the audience rose to their feet during the performance and they were cheering and applauding with such joy and veneration.

The reaction to a singer like Susan was overwhelming. Picture this folks. There it was, Raw Talent pulling in the audience with its immense power and musical singing ability. This is what it's all about.

This is beyond good or excellent. This is pure, crystal clear singing. Even to this day from time to time when I view the video seeing that awesome performance brings tears to my eyes.

After her audition the judges had this to say. Piers Morgan said when you stated that you wanted to be like Elaine Page there were many people laughing at you. Well no one is laughing at you now. Your performance was stunning. He recalled that he had never seen anything like it in the three years that he had been judging.

Amanda Holden said she was so thrilled with Susan's performance because she knew that there was a lot of negativity before she performed. I think we were all being very cynical and that's the biggest wake up call ever. I just want to say it was a complete privilege listening to that

The three judges all voted yes. Piers Morgan said it all when he stated "I'm giving the biggest yes I have ever given to anybody."

In this day and age when far too often more emphasis is put on looks, pizzazz and glitter, it's important to remember that the true core here is musical talent. As the expression goes, never judge a book by its cover but always by its content.

There is a seven minute You Tube video of Susan's first appearance on Britain's Got Talent. You will see something that some people will probably see only once in their lifetime.

Again, there's the picture of a woman singing. There's no pyrotechnics, no fancy dancing or jumping up around on stage, and she was dressed plainly with standard everyday clothing. But she didn't need any of that. She just stood there center stage and let her Raw Talent show itself proudly. What she did have and what made this beyond good or excellent was her awe inspiring singing.

Your Notes

Your Notes

11

Having a Hit Record

There are so many stumbling blocks that prevent one from having a Hit Record that it's a miracle if any artist can succeed in getting one.

Record labels can't seem to understand why sales are down and yet cannot comprehend the situation since they are part of the problem. When big business got into music several years ago and bought out some of the Record companies they changed how things were done. They promoted the artists that could bring in massive money and ignored all the others regardless of how good the others were.

If asked what they attribute their declining sales to they would blame the internet. It's amazing how they ignored the internet as it was steamrolling along with new concepts that would allow listeners to hear all sorts of music for free or at a very cheap price. And the music is more diversified than ever.

With the 'we know more than you' attitude big business continues to avoid being creative. Instead of diversity we only hear the Top 25 or so songs played and repeated in a continuous loop on the radio stations' Play List.

Back in the day radio stations were a hotbed of good music. This is because in addition to their own Play List they received plenty of demos from the record labels and even aspiring artists. Imagine a young person coming into a radio station and talking with a DJ like Wolfman Jack or Alan Freed. He or she would say they had a record and if the DJ liked it could he put it on the air and play it. If he did, Bingo, it went on the air and got played everyday without fail as long as listeners were still calling in and saying how much they liked it. There was plenty of diversity then since if it was good music the DJ would play it and allow it in.

Many artists think of learning to play a music instrument or singing and being in a band. They think of playing at functions and clubs. They think about cutting a record or album and hopefully getting discovered.

It seems that the hidden trait for success here is that few artists think of the fact that if they ever want to reach the top line in the music industry and make some hit records then they must have a Platform (A good sized following of fans as a base). The Labels will not be interested unless they feel the fan base can generate sales.

Developing a fan base involves much planning and work and is something that should start early on in one's career. The reason to start early on is that Networking with the right people and promoting one's self is essential and can take a long period of time.

There are several opportunities to network. Going into music stores or even working there especially if they sell instruments or recording equipment. This is a prime chance to talk with musicians and others in the music business that will frequent the store.

Working at a radio station for low wages or as an intern is also a good place to network with people. When I was a Production Director at a large radio network they would have interns in. It was a great learning experience for them especially given that it was a Network and not just a single station environment.

Also working at a music publishing company or in a recording studio can provide many contacts in the business.

This also would apply to schools of music. If they are higher echelon schools such as Berklee in Boston or the Julliard School of Music in New York then that is all the better. If you can afford to take classes you should.

As with some things in life there can be a positive side to a situation. The following story is about how fate intervened in the lives of two songwriters.

Several years ago Elton John and Bernie Taupin had answered a newspaper ad for songwriters put out by Liberty Records. They had each applied separately but there was no interest in them individually.

However, fate was about to intervene. Ray Williams, an A&R man for Liberty was looking for new talent. He told Elton that a songwriter had been in and applied as Elton had but was not accepted for the position. Ray told Elton about Bernie and suggested that they might have enough in common to write songs together as a team. This seemed plausible as Bernie was a lyricist and Elton was a music composer.

The two eventually did get together and made songwriting history with memorable song hits such as "Rocket Man, Crocodile Rock, Bennie and the Jets" and so many more.

I mention this to show that if Elton and Bernie hadn't been open to networking then the chance encounter with Ray at Liberty possibly would have been a missed opportunity.

If you are a singer, songwriter or musician you must practice long hours daily and be ready to show your best stuff when an opportunity presents itself.

In regards to moving on *Up the Ladder of Success*, the higher you want to go the harder you'll have to work. If you are going for the Queen's Jewels you will be breathing, singing and living everything about music day in and day out.

The important thing is that with all your hard work you can also be having fun in your love affair with music. In turn it will bring lasting memories and smiles to all.

Your Notes

Your Notes

Part Four

"Internet awaits and lessons to be
learned from the Greats"

12

Your Music: Internet to the Rescue

The following information is given to help any of you, whether you're a novice or long time music artist, to find inexpensive ways to sell your music.

Unfortunately the big four or five record companies are like used car dealers. They have a bad reputation and would look you right in the eye and say, "Gee, why would anyone think that we would do anything illicit."

Have no fear though. We're going to talk about the music business on the internet. As usual I'll give you some of the hidden traits that you need to know since I've personally been through it.

Let's start by first talking about the preparation and manufacturing of your product and end with the selling of the finished product which is your CD.

The preparation is first because anything else whether it is a website, one of the social networking sites, Word Press, selecting songs, manufacturing and marketing need to be built around the finished CD product.

Starting out you will need to record a completed and finished CD. But before doing that and this is important you must learn about Publishing Rights.

First you have to select the songs that you are going to put on the CD. If the song is a new one that you wrote the lyrics and/or music for, then you should by all means register it with a respective agency such as ASCAP or BMI. Also be sure and get it copyrighted with the United States Copyright office in Washington, DC.

However because the majority of the songs that artists record are cover songs of someone else's work, they are the ones that I will be talking about today.

The company that I use is the Harry Fox Agency out of New York City.

You need to obtain a Mechanical license and it should be a Limited Quantity one. That means that you can purchase it in varying quantities. To start with you should go for a small number like 200 or 250 as you will not know how many you will sell. The cost for that amount is quite small but if you need a larger quantity as in the thousands then the price would be more.

To start with you would search on the HF online data base for the song title you are interested in and the artist's rendition of that song that you want the license for. You will also see the Publisher(s) for the song.

The main thing to look for is to see if the license is available. If not, then you will not be able to get one for that song. This is why you would never record the songs first. The reason being that if you couldn't get the license then you would have to delete that recording and find a song to replace it. Obviously this is going to cost you time and money whereas if you get the license first you are ready to go.

The next thing that you will need to do is find a studio to record in. But before doing that you must take the selected songs you received your license for and practice and fine tune them many times over before you ever go into a recording studio. Remember you MUST be prepared with your music before going into the studio to do your songs.

I want to relate a story here that affirms the importance of finding the right studio. There was a local country music band that I had seen perform on occasion which I felt was a very good band. They had years of experience playing at different clubs.

I had heard that they had recorded a CD and I was interested to buy one when it came out. This was based on hearing their music at several different places that they played at.

Finally the day arrived and I anxiously purchased the CD and then got a chance to listen to it. I can only say that it was a mediocre recording at best. It really didn't sound like them at all. Since I knew what they sounded like in person, the poor quality showed that it was not recorded in a good studio.

Therefore when you are searching for a studio along with the cost of the studio time, be sure to ask them for some samples of their recordings. And preferably ones that are of the music genre that you are in.

Remember that when looking for a studio to record in there is no need to make a commitment at the time. Honesty is the best policy. Just tell them that you are looking at studios to see which one would be best for you and your group to record in.

If you look at three different studios then you will have a pretty good idea of what is being offered and the costs involved.

When they give you the hourly cost for renting the recording studio, be sure to ask if that includes the engineer or production person that runs the controls. Also ask if there are any additional costs associated with the session.

Be sure that if you have any questions to write them down ahead of time so that you can ask them during your discussion about costs.

A brief word about DIY is in order. If one had Pro Tools and could record, there are things to consider. If it is being done in a home studio does it have the sound proofing and control area set up room-wise that would be comparable to a commercial recording studio.

It's so important to not forget about Quality Assurance. Remember the master CDs are going to be made from the recording and you need the best quality possible for the finished product that you want to sell. A Master CD is what you will give to the Manufacturing or

Production company that will fulfill your order for the initial CD production run.

With that said it is important that you ask the recording studio for Replicated master CDs. Do not accept Duplicate copies from the recording studio. They may be less expensive but the quality is less also. So remember Replicate is the word and be sure you get spares for backup if needed.

Before continuing on, it's important that you know I do not receive any compensation for mentioning various companies in this book. They are companies that I do business with on a regular basis and am satisfied with their products.

You are having the advantage here of an author that actually uses these products rather than like some authors that have never used them and are relating them to something that they have read about in trade publications.

Now back to the process. Once you have your finished CD you will need peripheral things to be given to the manufacturing company besides the Master CDs.

In all probability you will need to hire a graphic artist who is familiar with CD Cover work. Your CD Cover art and its packaging are important as it is the first image a customer sees of your product. The Cover art can be a stock photo or an original that you shoot and all text needs to be formatted for fonts. There is also printing that needs to be done right on the top of the CD. Things such as Song Titles, Publisher and any other information that you want can go there. If you wish there are also some manufacturing firms that do this graphic work.

You can learn a tremendous amount of knowledge simply by going into a store's CD section and see what other CDs look like. If you see something that you like design wise you could buy it, open it up and thoroughly explore the cover jacket back to and including the tray card and then show it to the graphic artist as an example of what you would be interested in.

There are some artists that would prefer to give the project to someone and let them do the whole thing including picking out the design and all. The one thing that can be said about that is if you really care about your product then you've got to be willing to get involved in it and participate in the project.

You will also need a UPC Bar Code which must be put on the back of the tray card cover. The production company can supply you with one for a small fee. They will print it on the back of your tray card. Retail stores will require it as the code has information on your product that is unique to it.

The ideal company and the one I use for the Production of CDs is called Disc Makers. Their main headquarters are in New Jersey and they have administrative satellite offices around the country.

The benefits to using this company are somewhat amazing. First of all they are and beyond a full-service company. They manufacture your completed CDs including the graphic artist's work. Not only do they have a large sample of Jewell cases, Digipaks, and Eco-wallet jackets, but they can manufacture a small order of finished CDs for someone just starting or a large amount in the thousands for an artist that is moving on up.

Their product line also includes DVD manufacturing and they even have automated disc duplication and replication print machines for the Do It Yourself folks.

They also have their own fulfillment house for shipping your product to just about anywhere.

And if that isn't enough they have their own design house and provide a Professional Mastering service under the Sound Lab there at the plant for your music project. Everything I have mentioned takes place under one roof at their plant in New Jersey.

Up to now everything that I have mentioned can be managed by you or you can outsource it and hire people to do it for you.

The advantage to DIY is that you learn more particulars about the whole process and in certain scenarios you can save money. The disadvantage is that you eat up so much time that it's almost more practical to outsource some of it as in the case of the graphics art work.

You will also find that there can be quite a bit of paperwork to be filled out for getting the publishing rights at the Harry Fox Agency and your disc manufacturing process at Disc Makers.

I realize that this can be quite daunting and it does require a lot of studying. But remember the title of this book and Steve Jobs and to never give up with your persistence. You can do it! I've been through it so I know what it's like.

Now at this point you have a completed CD and you've ordered a small run of units from Disc Makers. Finally it's time to market it for sale.

One way to market it is through the internet via places like iTunes, Amazon, and other services. It's important to remember that all of them charge a fee for allowing you to market your CD on their site.

Their fee usually averages 25% to 30% of the total selling price. So if you have the whole CD for sale for $10.00, then you would get $7.00 and they would get $3.00

If on the other hand you are selling single songs for .99¢ you would get .70¢ and they would get .30¢

S&H costs only apply to Physical CDs and not to Digital CDs.

Even if you decided to do it yourself on your own site you would need a payment collector service like PayPal or some other service. They would set-up a shopping cart and payment collection for customers to order your product. Besides their regular fee they also charge you a small transaction fee on the order. Since market pricing can vary from year to year you should check with any company that you are going to sell your product through to see what their current fees are.

One of the major downsides of using any of the internet sites such as iTunes to sell your products is they do not give you the email or shipping address of the purchasers. Hence you cannot build a list of customers. However a sale is a sale and it does produce income.

iTunes attitude is they are the largest seller of music on planet earth so with that type of exposure if you don't like it then you can go someplace else. Unfortunately the others are all pretty much the same as they will not give you the address and name of the people that buy your product through them.

One of the things that I found out about audio Podcasts in iTunes is that you cannot charge for them. That is why you will always see Free where there would be a price for those type products.

A hidden trait that I discovered is that Podcasts can be an ideal place to test to see if there is even interest in something that you are selling. So if you have a single cut on an album you could do a Podcast with it and see if there is any interest in it. Now remember it is Free so you are not getting anything but information from it.

Even though people that click on a product might not be a buyer it can be a barometer if someone has interest in it. I've used this on a product I had and it was a good measure that showed there was interest in it in certain locations.

The last thing that we should discuss here is how to get your CD product set up and for sale say on iTunes. Set-up is Free.

I discovered through them that as an artist you should have 20 albums in your catalog if you were going to do business with them on your own. When most artists see that information they get discouraged as they do not have 20 albums let alone one.

But I did find out that you do not need any previous albums before the one that you want to market if you go through an Apple approved Aggregator instead.

Aggregators are third parties that can help you meet the technical requirements, deliver and manage your content, and assist with marketing efforts. The technology is really complex to set up the products for sale on your own. This is why the aggregators are so useful. They've got it all to make it happen. Apple has a list of approved Aggregators in the iTunes Connect pages.

The company I use for aggregating my recording content into Apple's iTunes and others is CD Baby. They are actually owned by Disc Makers.

The process involves your applying to them and filling out the paperwork for your recorded CD. They then set it up including the price per cut and the price for the total album. They do this not only on iTunes but in all their other digital partners such as Amazon and the like. They do it all for you.

Remember the beauty of this is that it is your own product. You're an Independent. You decide where it goes, how much to charge and who sells it. There is no record label or producer as in a major label telling you what is or isn't and the part of your CD they own. 'You Own It.'

Don't forget to set-up your website as you need your product to have a home. Part of this process is to get a domain name first and register it with a Hosting company.

It is good to register the Domain name in both .com and .net. The one that I use is GoDaddy. I believe they are currently the largest retailer of Domain Names in the country.

The one thing that sets them apart from all the others is that for their website builders and domains they have 24/7 live support help.

PLUS you area not talking to someone in a foreign country that you cannot understand. The techs that you talk with are in California and Arizona and speak clearly and are quite knowledgeable.

Your Notes

Your Notes

13

Music Genres and their artists

As part of your musical journey you will have to pick a music genre style that you like and will enjoy singing or playing.

It's a known truth among artists that along with the learning curve of your choice that one should include a study of the Greats in your chosen genre. They have done it all and shown they are the tops in their field. So there is much to learn about your genre by listening to some of their recordings and if possible seeing any of their videos.

Besides seeing their mannerisms and phrasing when they sing before an audience or in a studio there is also an additional great benefit.

It is the possibility of hearing a song that you would like to record. Many of the songs today are cover songs. So there can be several recordings of one song title by other artists. Not everyone has a hit with those.

However you might hear something that says if it's arranged differently then you might be able to do something with it.

The following list is of artists by Genre who have contributed immensely to that style.

The line read is Artist, Album Title, and Release Year.

R&B

Michael Jackson: **Thriller** 1982

Aretha Franklin: **Lady Soul** 1968

Ray Charles: **Genius, The Ultimate Collection** 2009

Jimi Hendrix: **West Coast Seattle Boy** 2010

Mary J. Blige: **Growing Pains** 2007

Prince: **Purple Rain** 1984

Al Greene: **Let's Stay Together** 1972

Alicia Keys: **Girl on Fire** 2012

Bruno Mars: **Doo-Wops & Hooligans** 2010

Donna Summer: **The Journey** 2006

B.B. King: **Ladies and Gentlemen** 2012

Tina Turner: **Tina** 2008

Issac Hayes: **Hot Buttered Soul** 1969

Stevie Wonder: **Music of My Mind** 1972

Luther Vandross: **The Essential Luther Vandross**
2003

Lionel Richie: **The Definitive Collection** 2003

Boys II Men: **Legacy** 2001

Amy Whitehouse: **Frank** 2003

Pop/Rock

Queen: **A Night at the Opera** 1975

The Who: **The Who Sell out** 1967

The Beach Boys: **Sounds of Summer** 2003

The Rolling Stones: **Hot Rocks 1964-1971** 2002

Elvis Presley: **30#1 Hits** 2002

The Beatles: **1962-1966** 1973

Stevie Ray Vaughan: **Couldn't Stand the Weather**
1984

Eric Clapton: **Slowhand** 1977

Pink Floyd: **Dark Side of the Moon** 1973

Neil Diamond: **The Bang Years 1966-1968** 2011

Jerry Lee Lewis: **The Best of Jerry Lee Lewis** 2009

Leslie Gore: **The Golden Hits of Leslie Gore** 2008

The Ronettes: **Best of the Ronettes** 1992

Martha & The Vandellas: **The Definitive Collection** 2008

Allman Brothers **At Fillmore East** 1997

Bee Gees: **The Ultimate Bee Gees** 2009

Chuck Berry: **The Definitive Collection** 2006

Brenda Lee: **Definitive Collection** 2006

Dion & The Belmonts: **Greatest Hits** 1999

Bill Haley & His Comets: **Rock Around The Clock** 2004

James Brown: **20 All Time Greatest Hits** 1991

Carly Simon: **The Best of Carly Simon** 1990

Fats Domino: **The Fats Domino Jukebox** 2002

Duane Eddy: **Greatest Hits** (Import) 2006

The Everly Brothers: **All-Time Greatest Hits** 1990

Frankie Valli & The Four Seasons: **Greatest Hits 2** 1991

Carole King: **Tapestry** 1999

Little Richard: **Greatest Gold Hits** 2004

Roy Orbison: **Black & White Night** 2006

Neil Sedaka: **Definitive Collection** 2007

The Shirelles: **20 Greatest Hits** 2009

Simon & Garfunkel: **Simon and Garfunkel's**

Greatest Hits 1990

Diana Ross & The Supremes: **The #1's** 2004

Bruce Springsteen: **The Essential Bruce**

Springsteen 2003

Jackie Wilson: **20 Greatest Hits** 2002

New Age

Enya: **Only Time, The Collection** 2002

Yanni: **Live at the Acropolis** 1993

Steven Halpern: **Spectrum Suite** 1975

Celtic Women: **Songs From the Heart** 2010

Michael Hedges: **Breakfast in the Field** 1981

Bradley Joseph: **One Deep Breath** 2002

David Lanz: **Cristofori's Dream** 1988

William Ackerman: **Hearing Voices** 2001

RAP

The Beastie Boys: **Solid Gold Hits** 2005

Jay-Z: **American Gangster** 2007

Eminem: **Curtain Call** 2005

LL Cool J: **Mama Said Knock You Out** 1990

Tupac Shakur: **All Eyez on Me** 1996

The Notorious B.I.G.: **Ready to Die** 1994

Lil Wayne: **Tha Carter II** 2005

Pitbull: **The Boatlift** 2007

Classical

Andrew Lloyd Webber: **The Essential Songs of Andrew Lloyd Webber** 2002

Placido Domingo: **Amore Infinito** 2008

Original London Cast Recording: **Les Miserables** 1985

Columbia Symphony Orchestra: **Rhapsody in Blue** 1997

Leonard Bernstein: **1812, Festival Overture** 2004

Arthur Fiedler: **The Skaters' Waltz** 1999

Van Cliburn: **My Favorite Liszt** 2000

London Philharmonic: **The Marriage of Figaro.** 2006

London Symphony Orchestra: **Tchaikovsky:Nutcracker** 2006

Latin

Ricky Martin: **Ricky Martin** 1999

Jenni Rivera: **Joyas Prestadas** 2011

Enrique Iglesias: **Greatest Hits** 2008

Antonio Carlos Jobim/Elis Regina: **Elis & Tom** 1974

Selena: **Dreaming of You** 1995

Alejandro Fernandez: **Confidencias** 2013

Marc Anthony: **Vivir Mi Vida** 2013

Carlos Santana: **Santana** 1969

Ritchie Valens:**Ritchie Valens La Bamba** 1958

Shakira: **LaTortura** 2005

Blues

Etta James: **At Last** 1961

John Mayall: **Blues Breakers with Eric Clapton** 2001

B.B. King: **The Best of B.B. King** 1973

Jimmi Hendrix: **Blues** 1994

Gary Clark, Jr.: **Blak and Blu** 2012

John Lee Hooker: **Best of JLH** 2004

Bobby Parker: **Watch Your Step** 1961

Robert Cray: **Strong Persuader** 1986

Buddy Guy: **Buddy Guy and Junior Wells Play the Blues** 1972

Willie Clayton: **Something to Talk About** 1998

Sean Costello: **We Can Get Together** 2008

Muddy Waters: **Muddy Mississippi Waters Live** 1979

Reggae

Bob Marley and The Wailers: **Original Cuts** 2004

Steel Pulse: **Reggae Fever** 1980

Jimmy Cliff: **Jimmy Cliff** 1969

Shaggy: **Boombastic** 1995

Derrick Morgan: **Tougher Than Tough** 1992

The Clarendonians **Can't Keep a Good Man Down**
1992

Lucky Dube: **Serious Reggae** 1996

Jah Cure **Freedom Blues** 2005

Country

Johnny Cash: **Original Sun Singles 54-58** 2009

George Jones: **I Am What I Am** 1980

Dolly Parton: **The Essential Dolly Parton** 2005

Emmylou Harris: **Songbird, Rare Tracks** 2007

Toby Keith: **35 Biggest Hits** 2008

Blake Shelton: **Pure BS** 2007

George Strait: **Troubadour** 2008

Alan Jackson: **Good Time** 2008

Reba McEntire: **50 Greatest Hits** 2008

Taylor Swift: **Fearless** 2008

Willie Nelson: **One Hell of a Ride** 2008

Kenny Rogers: **The Best of Kenny Rogers** 2008

Dwight Yoakam: **Dwight Sings Buck** 2007

Vince Gill: **Guitar Slinger** 2011

Jim Reeves: **Jim Reeves Greatest Hits** 2000

Buck Owens: **The Very Best of Buck Owens, Vol.1**
1994

Patsy Cline: **Patsy Cline's Greatest Hits** 2003

Alabama: **My Home's in Alabama** 1980

Statler Brothers: **Pardners in Rhyme** 1985

Lefty Frizzell: **Listen to Lefty** 1952

Gene Watson: **Eighteen Greatest Hits** 1999

Hank Williams: **The Essential Hank Williams** 1969

Merle Haggard: **Big City** 1981

Dottie West: **Wild West** 1981

Loretta Lynn: **Coal Miner's Daughter** 1970

Ray Price: **For The Good Times** 1970

Conway Twitty: **Hello Darlin'** 1970

Charley Pride: **Charley Pride's 10th Album** 1970

Eddy Arnold: **My World** 1965

Jazz

Dave Brubeck: **Time Out** 1959

Miles Davis: **Kind of Blue** 1959

Sonny Rollins: **Road Shows, Vol.1** 2008

Herbie Hancock: **Maiden Voyage** 1965

Omette Coleman: **The Shape of Jazz to Come** 1959

Diana Krall: **Love Scenes** 1997

Duke Ellington: **The Complete Capitol Recordings** 1999

Ella Fitzgerald: **Twelve Nights in Hollywood** 2009

Louis Armstrong: **Struttin'** 1996

Dizzy Gillespie: **At Newport** 1957

Billie Holiday: **The Complete Billie Holiday** 1994

Count Basie: **Basie and Eckstine Incorporated** 1959

John Coltrane: **Coltrane Jazz** 1961

Easy Listening

Dean Martin: **Dean Martin's Greatest Hits** 2000

Perry Como: **All Time Greatest Hits** 1990

Frank Sinatra: **Nothing But the Best** 2008

Al Martino: **Capital Collectors Set** 1992

Patti Page: **Golden Hits** 1960

Paul Anka: **The Very Best of Paul Anka** 2000

Rosemary Clooney: **Showcase of Hits** 2009

Frankie Lane: **Mule Train** 1989

Nat King Cole: **The Very Best of Nat King Cole** 2006

Bobby Darin: **The Ultimate Bobby Darin** 1988

Connie Francis: **20th Century Masters** 1999

Della Reese: **Voice of an Angel** 1990

Dusty Springfield: **20th Century Masters** 1999

Los Indios Tabajaras: **Maria Elena** 1964

Andy Williams: **16 most Requested Songs** 1986

Engelbert Humperdinck: **20th Century Masters** 2005

Judy Garland: **20th Century Masters** 1999

Tony Bennett: **The Ultimate Tony Bennett** 2000

Pat Boone: **Pat Boone's Greatest Hits** 1962

Anne Murray: **The Best of Anne Murray** 1994

Frankie Avalon: **The Best of Frankie Avalon** 2007

Judy Collins: **The Very Best of Judy Collins** 2001

Karen Carpenter: **Singles 1969-1981** 2000

Jackie Gleason: **Music For Lovers Only** 1952

Percy Faith: **Greatest Hits** 1960

Johnny Mathis: **The Best of Johnny Mathis** 1980

Dionne Warwick: **Dionne** 1979

Henry Mancini: **Breakfast at Tiffany's** 1962

Barbra Streisand: **People** 1964

Ray Conniff Singers: **Somewhere My Love** 1966

Doo-Wop

The Drifters: **All Time Greatest Hits** 2003

The Platters: **All Time Greatest Hits** 2004

The Five Satins: **The Original Master Tapes Collection, Vol.1 Fred Parris** 2006

The Four Tops: **Essential Collection** 2000

Kenny Vance: **Kenny Vance & The Planotones** 2002

The Moonglows: **Their Greatest Hits** 1997

Smokey Robinson & The Miracles: **The Ultimate Collection** 1998

The Vogues: **The Vogues Greatest Hits** 1990

Shep & The Limelites: **Daddy's Home to Stay** 1998

Jay & The Americans: **Greatest Hits** 1995

The Duprees: **All Time Greatest Hits** 2002

The Heartbeats: **A Thousand Miles Away** 2005

The Crystals: **Best of the Crystals** 1992

The Flamingos: **Best of The Flamingos** 1990

Johnny Maestro & The Crests: **20 All-Time**

Greatest Hits 2001

The Fleetwoods: **The Very Best of The Fleetwoods**

1993

Little Anthony & The Imperials: **25 Greatest Hits**

1998

The Diamonds: **21 Carats All The Hits** 2005

Jimmy Clanton: **The Best of Jimmy Clanton,**

Venus in Blue Jeans 2009

Ronnie Dove: **Golden Classics** 1994

The Tokens: **Wimoweh!! The Best of The Tokens**

1993

The Chiffons: **Sweet Talkin' Girls The Best of the**

Chiffons 2006

The Penguins: **Earth Angel** 1990

The Original Chantels: **There's Our Song Again**
1962

The Charts: **The Charts Greatest Hits** 1981

The Orioles: **Sing Their Greatest Hits** 1969

The Spaniels: **The Very Best of the Spaniels** 2009

The Solitaires: **Still Walking Along** 2007

The Dubs: **The Best of the Dubs** 1991

The Mystics: **The Mystics Greatest Hits** 2010

Kathy Young: **The Very Best of Kathy Young** 2011

The Fireflies: **You Were Mine** 1961

The Coasters: **The Very Best of the Coasters** 2009

Gerry and the Pacemakers: **The Very Best of** 2008

Herman's Hermits: **Their Greatest Hits** 1990

The Lovin' Spoonful **Greatest Hits** 2000

Gene Chandler: **Nothing Can Stop Me: Greatest
Hits** 1994

The Byrds: **Greatest Hits** 2008

Folk

Kingston Trio: **Kingston Trio Greatest Hits** 2011

Peter, Paul & Mary: **Very Best of Peter, Paul &**

Mary 2005

Peter & Gordon: **The Ultimate Peter & Gordon**

2001

Woody Guthrie: **This Land is Your Land: The**

Asch Recordings, Vol.1 1997

Chad & Jeremy: **Very Best of Chad & Jeremy** 2000

The Rooftop Singers: **Best of The Rooftop Singers**

1993

Pete Seeger: **Pete Seeger's Greatest Hits** 2002

Gale Garnett: **We'll Sing in The Sunshine** 1998

The Irish Rovers: **The Best of The Irish Rovers**

1990

Your Notes

Your Notes

*Louis Armstrong was once asked about
different genres of music. He said that 'genres
are a guide to styles of music but in reality there
are only two types of music.*
Good Music and Bad Music'

Tracking Your Recordings

I want to be sure that you have information on two very important organizations. The first one is known as

ASCAP, The American Society of Composers, Authors, and Publishers.

ASCAP is the only member-owned performance rights organization in the U.S.

Their purpose is to insure that you get paid when your music is played.

Your processing fee for the application is $50.00 and there are no annual dues.

ASCAP is the first U.S. performing rights organization to distribute royalties for performances on the internet.

ASCAP states that they collect significantly more money from music users for performing rights than any other organization in the world. They claim that every penny they collect, less operating costs is distributed to members. More than .88¢ of each dollar they collect goes right back to members in royalties.

I encourage you to visit their website ASCAP.com for a wealth of information about their Society.

BMI, Broadcast Music, Incorporated is the second organization that I want to mention. BMI was started by the National Association of Broadcasters in 1939. They were founded later than ASCAP which was formed in 1914.

Their functions and services performed are quite similar to each other. Both BMI and ASCAP are considered a PRO which is a (Performance rights organization).

Originally BMI focused on radio station royalties but did expand over time to many other areas similar to ASCAP's.

There are only minor differences between the two such as writers can only affiliate with one society.

I encourage you to visit their website BMI.com for a tour of their enterprise as you hopefully did with ASCAP.

After that you can choose the organization that suits your needs best.

About the Author

Professional

Broadcasting: Paul Romaine has been involved in radio broadcasting as a Production Director for a large radio network. This involved managing the recordings of several people required to do voice work to air on the master Play List.

Podcasting: Paul has several audio Podcast commentaries in iTunes as well as Celebrity Interviews. They cover celebrity singers, songwriters, and musicians. His Podcasts are heard in over 88 countries worldwide

Radio Show Host: Currently Paul spends a portion of his time in developing a new show. It is a Talent Search for Singers, Songwriters and Musicians. It can be found at the following address:
http://www.SingersandMusiciansTalentSearch.com

Writer: Paul is a published writer in Ezine Articles and several E-book articles in Amazon.

Personal

TAD Quite often your articles and audio commentaries seem to appeal to readers. Any secrets why they do so well?

PR I feel that one of the reasons is the outline that I use to write them.

- I only write about Singers, Songwriters and Musicians.
- I have to like their work to begin with.
- I am not a music critic so my articles are positive rather than negative.
- I give some standard information about the celebrity that the reader may or may not know. But the most important thing is that I try to insert some positive traits that I discover about the singer's character that I find meritorious.

TAD You seem to write about a variety of music genres. Is there any particular reason for that?

PR Mainly to satisfy as many readers as possible. There is no such thing as a style of music or an artist that will appeal to everyone. So I spread it out in terms of music genres. Examples of that are:

- Younger pop stars such as Bruno Mars, Lady Gaga and Jennifer Lopez to older stars such as Frank Sinatra, Dean Martin and Neal Diamond.
- Hip-Hop artists like Jay-Z and LL Cool J
- Classical artists like, Jackie Evancho,

- Country artists like Patsy Cline, Alan Jackson and Toby Keith
- Rock and Rollers like James Brown, Jerry Lee Lewis and Little Richard
- And finally a lady that has that very rare thing known as Raw Talent, Susan Boyle

TAD What is your favorite genre of music?
PR For me, hands down it's romantic ballads, Love songs for slow dancing.

TAD If you had your choice to do anything work-wise in life that you wanted what would that be?
PR It would be what I am doing now. I just love music. I was around at the birth of Rock and Roll so in all these years I've seen a lot of varied music genres peak and drop. One thing for certain though is they still shine because they had so many great hits.

I read books about music all the time because there's so much to learn about our beloved music profession. It's almost a sin to love music and all its peripheral things as much as I do.

Recently I read a fascinating biography about one of the greatest songwriters of all time, Irving Berlin. It was a large book that talked about the birth of plays and musicals on Broadway in New York in the early 1900s. It even went back before that and afterward took the reader through many decades of music up until Irving's death in 1989. Every book about music can be a wonderful history lesson of the time period when it was written.

There were other books that provided a history lesson about racism against black singers in the beginning stages of Rock and Roll. No matter what the information is about it educates us as to what was going on with music at that time.

For example some white singers would record hit songs that black singers had recorded. This gave the white singers an advantage since air play for black singers was minimal compared to that for white singers.

A friend recently told me that "in regards to the hit song "Tutti Frutti" we didn't want to hear Pat Boone's version. We wanted to hear Little Richard's version."

In 2012 *Rolling Stone* magazine stated that "Tutti Frutti still contains what has to be considered the most inspired rock lyric ever recorded." Who could ever forget Little Richard singing one of the most famous rock lyrics in the history of music?

"a-wop-bop-a-loo-bop-a-lop-bam-boom."

WEB SITES

www.PaulRomaine.com
www.TalentSearchRadio.com
www.UpTheDownLadderOfSuccess.com

"Memorable great music will return when the formula that has already proved it can happen is allowed to return"

Acknowledgments

It takes many support people to bring about the completion of a book. In no particular order I'd Like to thank the following:

- Amazon for their patience and motivation
- Microsoft Office Word for their tech support
- Harry, my best friend forever
- TAD Publications for their loyalty during this project and others

And finally the people that we rarely see acknowledged in books but I can never forget are all our 'Friends in Music' who purchase this book.

"Good Music Lasts a Lifetime"

Made in the USA
Charleston, SC
27 February 2014